Hello Everyone

I'm Symone. My Spirit Name is MeritHebai Ashash-t, which means (Merit (Love) Hebai (Playfulness) Ashash-t (flowers). I also go by Mona or Selexa as well. Thank you for taking the time out of your day to glimpse into my World. You're really going to Enjoy this book. Have Fun!!

Question: What does it mean to be healthy to you?

Question: What do you think makes a Child most Happy?

Question: What do you think is one thing that someone should
Accomplish in Life?

Question: What is an Example of making Progress?

Question: Why would some Children Argue with One Another?

Question: What is one thing you could do to help or assist with your Generation?

Question: What do you want to do Tomorrow and what did you do Yesterday?

Question: If you could become anything in Life, what would it Be?

Question: What does the World look like to You?

Question: Is there anything you would Change about the World
you see?

Question: How Do you feel about Yourself?

Question: Why do you feel the way you do about Yourself?

Question: What does Meditation mean to You?

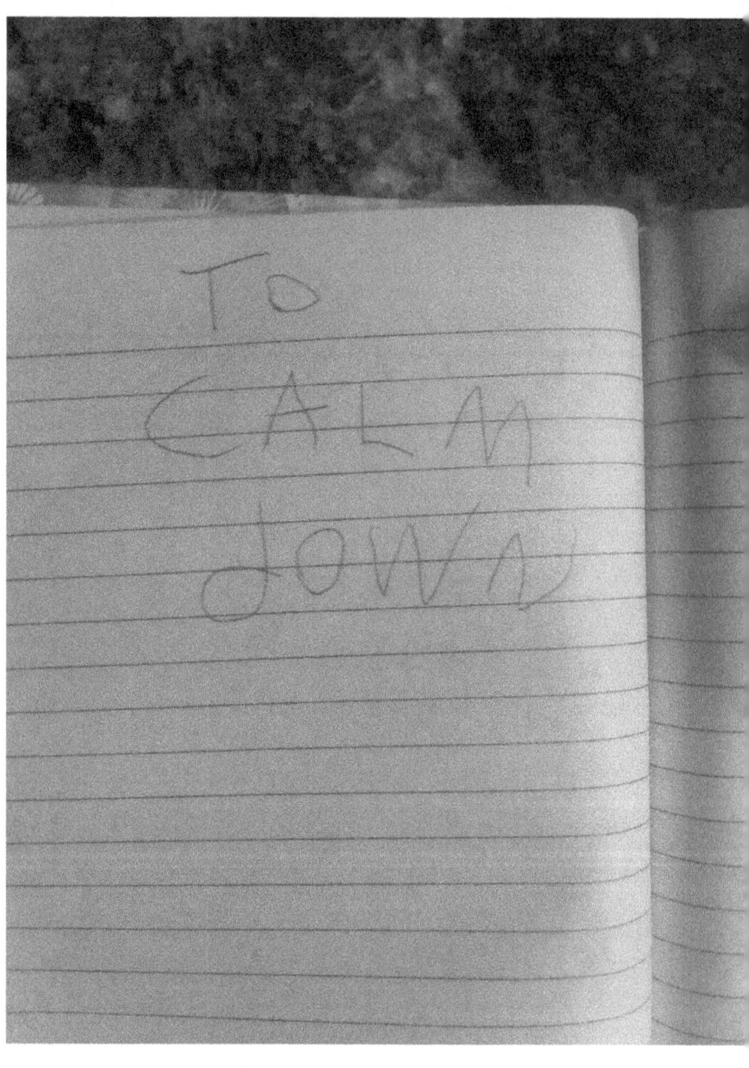

Question: Are you Powerful?

Question: What is your favorite Talent that you Have?

Question: What is a Friend to You?

Question: Does your Family all look the Same?

Question: When are you most Tired?

Question: What's Happening Right Now?

Question: Can a Family be too Big?

Question: How do you feel about Gaia (Earth)?

Question: How do you think Gaia (Earth) Feels?

Question: Do you think an Animal can be your Friend? If so,
then why?

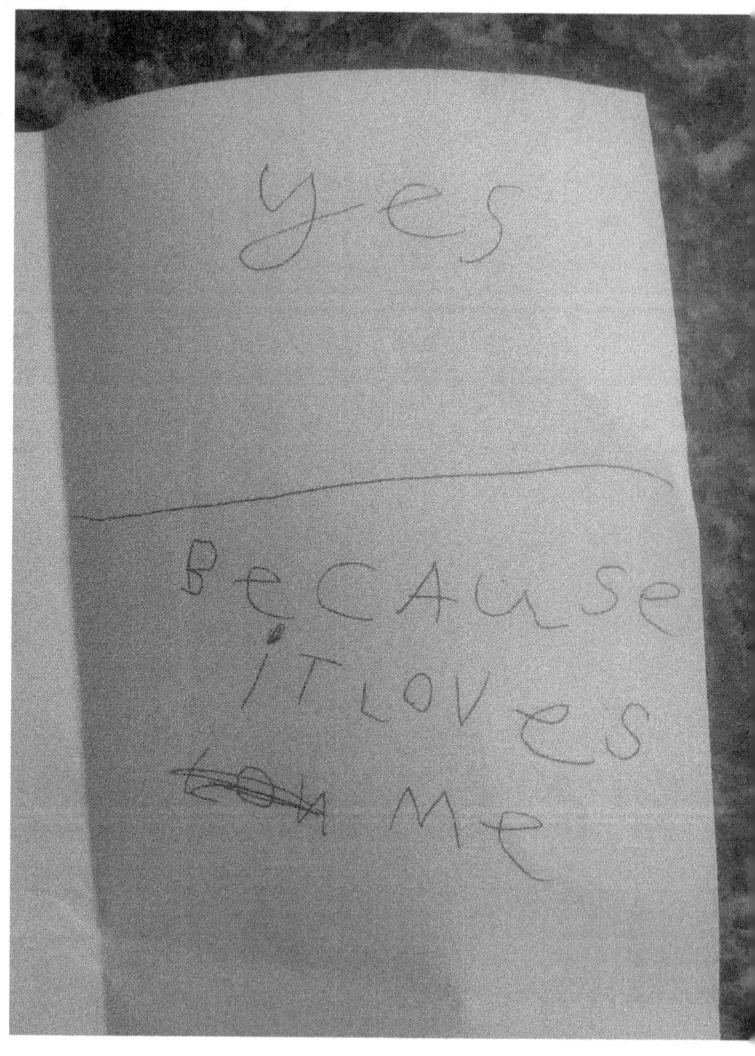

Question: Do you think Nature has Feelings? What do you think Nature Feels?

Question: Now, How do you Feel?

Question: Why do you think you're being asked these
Questions?

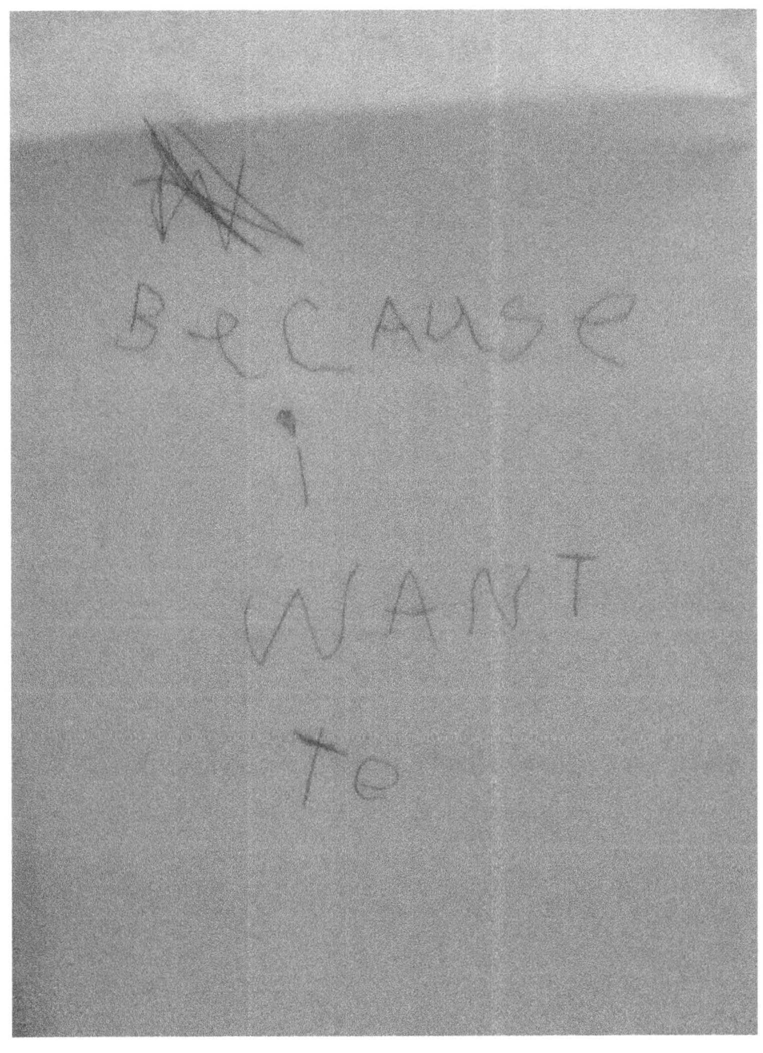

Question: How do these Questions make you Feel?

Question: Can you have more than 1 place you call Home? If So
then Why?

Question: What is Life to you?

Question: What does transition mean to you?

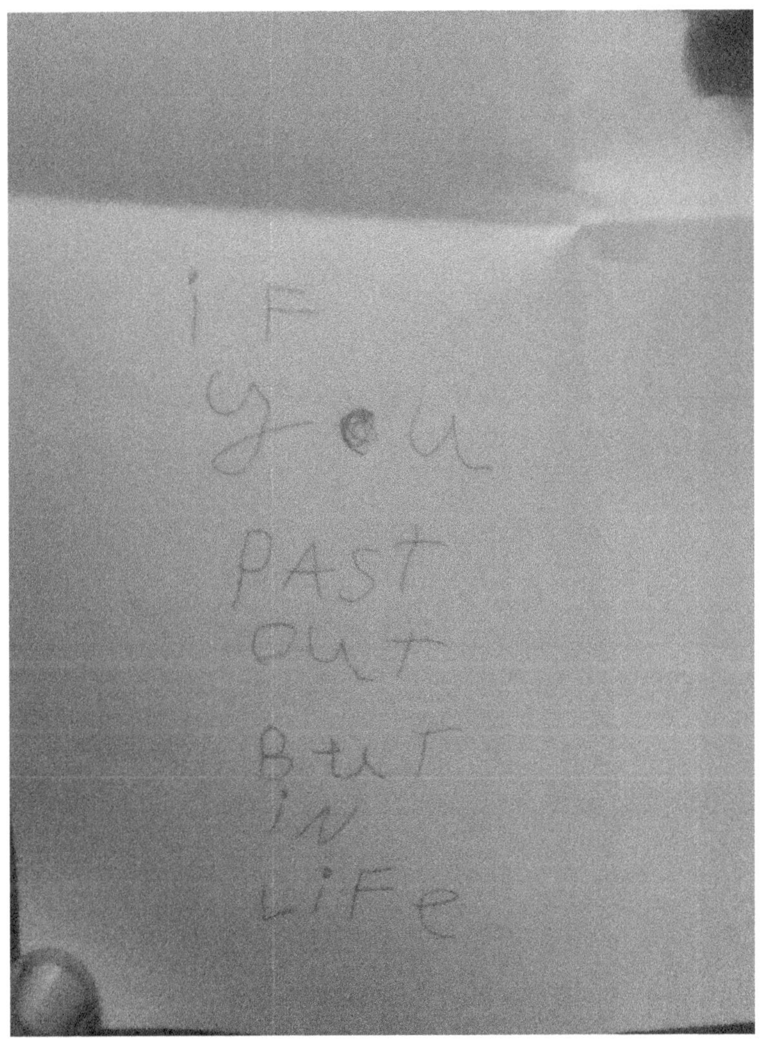

Question: What is Love to You?

To be Continued....

Writer: Symone Daniel (MeritHebai Ashash-t)

Illustration Coordinator: Ayeri Nyah Assom

Editor: UraeusAmaru O. AnuwiHeruUr

Editor Commentary/Notes: All Mona's (Selexa) answers were written 10/15/2020-10/21/2020 Gregorian calendar, 02/05/2013-02/11/2013 Ethiopian calendar. She is currently in her 8th year of life in this incarnation. As a blossoming young seedling, her depth of feeling is an immense unique kind. The Intention of this book is to bring back together seemingly 2 different modalities. One of Critical thinking Analysis and the other Pure Creativity thru creative expression. However, it also is a reminder to us all, to allow the next generation to express themselves Freely, without any kind of judgement for what they may feel, see, or want to express. These Children that are entering into our Plane are very Powerful with Untapped Potential. So, let us all remember, to perceive our realities as well as others thru the lens of an Innocent Child!

<u>Cheat Sheet</u>:

Question: What is a friend to you?

 Answer-Mona has a Friend named Nine

Question: What does it mean to be Healthy to you?
Answer-Fruits and Vegetables

Question: What is Life to you?

Answer- Ancestors